Karate-Do

The Art of Defense

T0149333

A.O. Mercado

iUniverse, Inc.
Bloomington

Karate-Do
The Art of Defense

iUniverse books may be ordered through booksellers or by contacting:

iUniverse
1663 Liberty Drive
Bloomington, IN 47403
www.iuniverse.com
1-800-Authors (1-800-288-4677)

ISBN: 978-1-4759-1035-3 (sc)
ISBN: 978-1-4759-1036-0 (ebk)

Library of Congress Control Number: 2012906260

Printed in the United States of America

iUniverse rev. date: 05/24/2012

Table of Contents

Grandmaster Austin Box, inducted member of the United States Martial Arts Hall of Fame (2009, Native American Grandmaster of the Year).

Foreword

My relationship with A.O. Mercado started in the early years of his karate training when he first attended my dojo in Colorado Springs, Colorado. I recall that he was among the three Midwest region finalists selected to represent the Japan Karate Association (JKA) to compete for the 1975 World Karate-Do Championship - U.S. Elimination at Los Angeles, California.

After many years of karate training, he was promoted and considered one of my top five black belt instructors.

When I visited the Kansas City dojo, I noticed that each one of his students had a training manual. After reviewing the training manual, I immediately decided to implement its use for all the members of the Hana - Dai Ichi Karate Association. KARATE-DO: The Art of Defense, in Chapter Eight, has a model training program which A.O. developed and included in the manual.

The book is a direct result of what he had acquired as a martial artist and U.S. Army Military Combative Instructor.

In addition to his teaching position at the Kansas City dojo, he holds various martial arts seminars in the Midwest - Kansas, Missouri, Nebraska and Iowa.

The practicing beginner or advanced karateka will find the foundation provided in this book an invaluable source to obtain a first degree black belt or higher.

Austin Box
10th Degree Grandmaster
Founder, Hana-Dai Ichi Karate Association

"Blessed be the Lord my strength, which teacheth my hands to war, and my fingers to fight:" Psalm 144:1

Preface

I have been approached by university and YMCA students who have asked me what is the appropriate karate book to purchase. I am aware that there are several informative karate books in the market today. However, some of these books deal only with the introduction and fundamentals of karate.

My purpose in writing <u>KARATE-DO: The Art of Defense</u> is to utilize the book as a textbook for the dojo and university students. This book covers a plurality of the karate fundamentals. In addition, this book has two chapters that I consider very unique. Chapter II (Diagram and Medical View of the Vital Points) informs the practitioner of the combative and safety points. Chapter X (Nutrition Produces Performance) deals with the benefits of nutrition to the karate practitioner and also to the person interested in the value of nutrition.

この本は、神への捧げものです。

Acknowledgements

First of all I would like to express my gratitude to the Lord for directing and providing the "Instruments" to accomplish writing this book.

I acknowledge my appreciation to the following people, without whom this book would not have been possible.

Irene L. Mercado, my wife, for her solid support,
Takamasa Morita, A.J. Mercado and Scott Evans for many hours of demonstrating karate techniques in front of the camera lights,
Mark James for his photography expertise,
Anthony Jappa for his fine illustrations,
Sherri Artale and Paolo Artale for editing the manuscript,
Donald R. Hendrickson for interviewing me in Chapter X,
Dr. Steven C. Hannah, M.D., for his medical expertise in assisting me write Chapter II,
Jeffrey Cunningham for his typing, graphic and type design,
Orlan Hill for his art direction.

CHAPTER ONE

The History, Objectives and Dynamics of Karate-Do

Meaning and History of Karate-Do

Karate-Do (kah-rah-teh-do) is written with three Chinese characters. Kara 空 empty, Te 手 hand and Do 道 is defined as "empty handed way." As an art of self-defense, the weaponless practitioner is capable of defending himself and suppressing his assailant successfully.

The art of karate initially expanded in the various parts of the Orient. China, Okinawa, Japan and Korea had cultures, which were instrumental in the promotion of the art to their inhabitants.

Today, throughout the world millions of people; men, women and children of all ages are practicing the art of karate. Japan Karate Association is the main organization responsible for promoting Karate-do around the world.

Karate is believed to have originated in ancient China and later spread to the Ryukyu Islands. This was due to the geographical proximity of these two cultures. Eastern China and Okinawa are only separated by 720 sea kilometers of the East China Sea.

For many centuries a foreign trade passage existed between China and Okinawa. Chinese merchants traded crafts, copper, silver, brass, gold, gunpowder and agricultural products with the Okinawan inhabitants. In addition, large groups of Chinese settlers migrated to Okinawa for religious, cultural and social reasons. It is because of this passage that interaction occurred between the Chinese "Ch'uanfa" masters and the native Okinawan martial artists. The Okinawa martial artists took great interest and intermixed the Chinese and the native art "Tode" and called it "Okinawate."

In 1609, Okinawa was under the jurisdiction of Satsuma, a clan from southern Kyushu, Japan. The government of Japan decided to illegalize the possession of all weapons in Ryukyu Islands. Inhabitants found with the possession of weapons were severely punished. As a result, the Okinawan weaponless fighting methods flourished and provided for the development of the Okinawan martial art form of today.

Historians have revealed that in the latter half of the nineteenth century and the early part of the twentieth century there were several karate lectures and demonstrations in Naha and Shuri, on the Ryukyu Islands. Many prominent karate masters such as Choki Motobu, Kenwa Mabuni, Chotoku Kyan, Gichin Funakoshi and Chojun Miyagi performed these demonstrations. During this era a delegation of Japanese government martial artists decided to invite Okinawan martial artists to perform karate demonstrations in the mainland of Japan. Mr. Choki Motobu, founder of Kempo karate, was one of the most highly qualified candidates to represent the Okinawan martial artists. However, he declined because he wanted a representative who had knowledge of tradition and culture of the Japanese inhabitants. The man the Okinawan martial artists chose was Gichin Funakoshi, later known as "The Father of Modern Karate-Do," who was born in 1869 in Shuri, Okinawa. Mr. Funakoshi was also the founder of Shotokan karate. (This is the Japanese style of karate.) "Mr. Funakoshi was invited to come to Japan to teach because he had all of the manners, customs and language that Motobu lacked, and these cultural factors were of the utmost importance in teaching the socially and economically elite."[1]

---

[1] From *Okinawa Kempo: Karate-Jutsu on Kumite* by Choki Motobu. Copyright and Published November 10, 1977 by Ryukyu Imports Inc., Olathe, Kansas

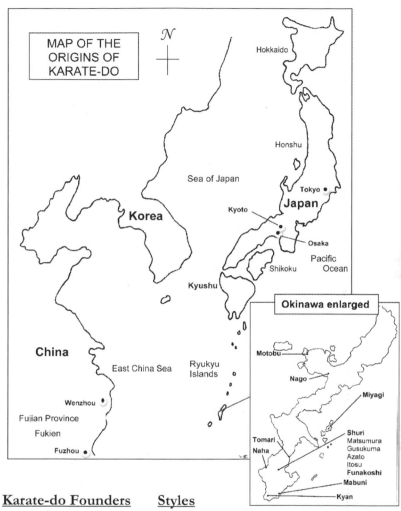

Karate-do Founders

Gichin Funakoshi
Choki Motobu
Kenwa Mabuni
Chotoku Kyan
Chojun Miyagi
Yasuhiro Konishi

Styles

Shotokan
Okinawan Kenpo
Shito-Ryu
Shorin-Ryu
Goju-Ryu
Shindo Jinen-Ryu

During 1912 through 1934, Mr. Gichin Funakoshi along with his disciples or students performed karate-do lectures and demonstrations in Tokyo, Kyoto, Osaka and Kyushu, Japan. There were many favorable comments concerning the demonstrations and immediately the demonstrations expanded throughout the Japanese mainland. High schools, universities and different organizations welcomed the demonstrations. Later the art was adopted by the Japanese high school and university curriculums. Many commercial dojos (halls or places) were established to promote the art to the Japanese people.

Objectives

There are many reasons why a person learns the art of karate. Let me explain two of the most common objectives, which are:

1. Self-defense.

2. Physical fitness.

In the aspect of self-defense, karate training if "mastered" is without equal. During the ancient times of the Orient, karate training was developed and taught secretly by the parents to their sons and daughters. One of the main reasons why the children learned the art was to protect themselves against aggressors who might subdue them and steal the family's property.

In the aspect of physical fitness, karate training enhances the practitioner's strength, endurance or wind, body coordination and weight control. The karate-ka (practitioner) has abundant energy to dispense as he encounters mental and physical tasks. Participation in karate training will also assist the karate-ka to relieve daily stresses of life.

Other objectives for karate training are:

1. Self-control.

2. Self-determination.

3. Self-discipline.

4. Self-perseverance.

Dynamics

Reaction Force

Newton's Third Law states "Every action (force) is accompanied by an equal and opposite reaction (force)."[2] Newton's Third Law is highly applied in karate training. For example: In executing a punch, the left hand is extended forward while the right hand is on the hip area. The left extended hand determines the force of the right forward punch. (The withdrawal of the left hand is the action and the right forward punch is the opposite reaction.)

Concentration of Power

The vast number of muscles should be coordinated to function together into executing a given technique.

In karate training you will hear the term "move by body." For example, when executing a kick, do not rely only on your foot. However, utilize the whole body as a weapon.

Breathing

In the inhaling phase, breathe in through the nose and the body muscles should be relaxed. In contrast the exhaling phase is a continuing contraction and tensing of the muscles.

While practicing karate, inhale prior to the execution of a technique and sharply exhale at the moment of execution. Then inhale normally after the technique has been completed (the relaxation phase of the movement).

---

[2] *From the Graphic of Survey by Taffel, (Oxford Book Co., New York, N.Y., 1960, p. 91).*

水の心

Mizu no kokoro

"The mind must be calm at all times, like the pond undisturbed."

Japanese Maxim

CHAPTER TWO

Diagram and Medical View of the Vital Points

The term vital point 急所 refers to any area of the human body that is susceptible of being incapacitated by a direct attack.

Vital points are classified into three areas:

1. High level: Skull and neck.

2. Middle level: Front, side and back of chest.

3. Lower level: Lower trunk.

It is imperative that all serious practitioners should familiarize themselves with the locations of these vital points. Knowing where these vital points are will enhance their chances of subduing the assailant in less time.

DIAGRAM OF KARATE VITAL POINTS

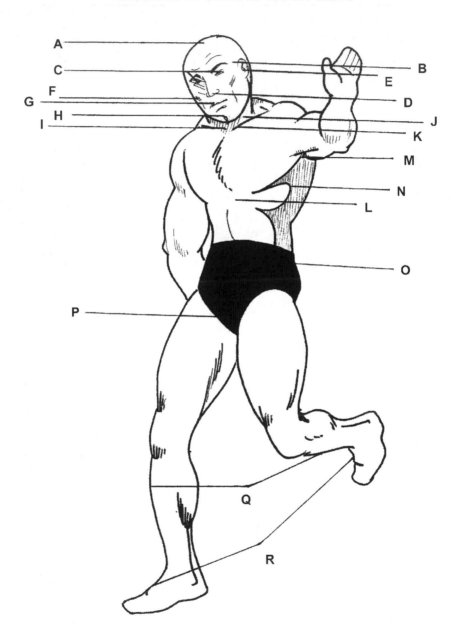

FRONT SIDE

A. Skull

B. Temple

C. Eyes

D. Nose

E. Ears

F. Jaw

G. Philtrum

H. Chin

I. Front of Neck

J. Side of Neck

K. Clavicle

L. Solar Plexus

M. Armpit

N. Floating Ribs

O. Abdomen

P. Groin

Q. Shin

R. Instep

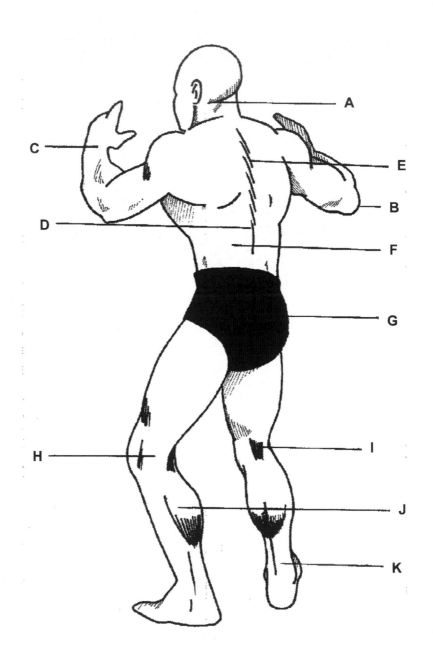

BACK SIDE

A. Base of Skull

B. Outside Elbow

C. Inner Wrist

D. Small of the Back

E. Upper Back

F. Kidney

G. Coccyx

H. Leg Joint

I. Hollow of the Knee

J. Calves

K. Achilles' Heel

Medical View of the Vital Points

The following is a medical view of the vital points most commonly used in karate. Each is followed by a brief explanation of why it is susceptible to injury and what would be the likely consequences of a blow struck to that area.

HEAD AND NECK

A. Skull:
As you know, the skull contains the brain. A hard blow to any area of the skull will probably result in unconsciousness. This is known as a concussion. A very hard blow could break the skull bone, bruise the brain or tear the brain from the blood vessels that supply it and cause death secondary to bleeding.

B. Temple:
This describes the area approximately 2 centimeters behind the corner of the eye. This overlies an area of the skull known as the pterion. A small blood vessel that supplies the covering of the brain with blood runs just under this point. It is called the middle meningeal artery. A hard blow to this area would disrupt this artery and cause fatal bleeding into the skull. The batting cap of baseball players has a piece of plastic extending down over the ear on the side facing the pitcher. This prevents a wild pitch from hitting the skull and damaging this artery.

C. Eyes:
A blow will result in either temporary or permanent blindness dependent upon the force of the blow. A very hard blow could rupture the eye causing severe pain and permanent blindness.

D. Nose:
The nose is made up of two small bones and several cartilages. A blow would cause pain and would probably fracture the nasal bones. Reflex tearing of the eyes also occurs, causing difficulty in seeing. It would be impossible to hit the nose and "drive the nasal bones into the brain" as it is sometimes said. The nasal bones are too short and the skull too strong to allow them to penetrate.

12

E. Ears:

A blow to the ears with the open hand would result in rupture (tearing) of the eardrum. This is very painful and would also result in temporary loss of hearing.

F. Jaw:

The lower jaw, also known as the mandible, is attached to the skull by a joint on both sides of the skull just in front of the ears. A blow to the side would most likely result in fracture to the mandible close to one of these joints. This causes severe pain and spasm of the muscles attaching to the jaw. A very hard blow would probably cause unconsciousness.

G. Philtrum:

This term refers to the area of the mouth just above the upper lip and just below the nose. It is also known as the maxilla. A hard blow would cause disruption of the front teeth and fracture of the bone. This would also probably result in loss of consciousness from shock to the brain.

H. Chin:

The chin is simply the front part of the mandible. A hard blow would result in fracture of the jaw in two places, one on each side where it meets with the skull. The results would be the same as striking the jaw (see above).

I. Front of Neck:

The front of the neck contains the windpipe, voice box, major arteries supplying blood to the brain and several important nerves. A blow could damage any of these structures and cause death. The swelling that would result from an injury could compress the windpipe and cause death from suffocation. This is a very vulnerable area of the human body.

J. Side of Neck:

The side of the neck consists mainly of muscle and nerves. A blow would cause severe pain from nerve injury and spasm of the muscles resulting in involuntary twisting of the neck. A very hard blow could fracture the bones in the spinal column causing paralysis or death from inability to breath. Soft tissue swelling could also compress the windpipe as described above.

FRONT SIDE

K. Clavicle:

The clavicle is another name for the collarbone. It is moderately thin and relatively easy to break. In addition, the major artery that supplies the arms runs underneath along the middle portion of the shaft. A strong blow could cause rupture of this artery resulting in severe bleeding, shock and possibly death.

L. Solar plexus:

The solar plexus is an old term for the area of the abdomen just below the end of the breastbone. Deep to this area is a collection of nerves known now as the celiac and superior mesenteric ganglia. These nerve collections provide innervations to almost all of the organs in the abdomen. When a blow is struck in this area, it causes extra impulses to travel down these nerves. One of the effects is that the body is "fooled" into thinking that there is a lot of air in the lungs. This causes the respiratory muscles (especially the diaphragm) to relax. Thus the person tries to take in a breath and cannot because his respiratory muscles are temporarily paralyzed. This is the feeling of having the "wind knocked out" of you. A very hard blow could tear the liver, stomach, aorta, pancreas, or kidney causing serious internal bleeding and possibly death.

M. Armpit:

The armpit, or axilla, contains the major nerve plexuses and blood vessels that supply the arm. A blow in this area would possibly tear these vessels and nerves causing numbness, or paralysis in the arm. Dislocation of the humerus, or arm bone, from the shoulder could also occur.

N. Floating ribs:

The human body contains twenty-four ribs, twelve on each side. The first ten on each side are attached to the spinal column in back and the breast bone and adjacent ribs in front. The last two ribs are called floating because they are not attached to anything in front. They are shorter than the other ribs and only reach to the side of the abdomen.

They are considered vulnerable because they partly overlay the kidneys. A blow to this area could fracture these ribs and cause secondary injury to the kidneys.

O. Abdomen:
The area between the chest and pelvis. A blow to this region can compress the intestine between the spine and striking body part resulting in intestinal damage.

P. Groin:
The groin is very susceptible to injury. A hard blow to the testicles can cause nausea and vomiting, or even unconsciousness from pain. Bleeding into the scrotum causes severe swelling and pain for days. The area behind the scrotum contains the urethra. A hard blow to this area can disrupt the urethra causing urine to spill into the soft tissues of the abdominal cavity. This causes infections and irritation of the tissues.

Q. Shin:
The shin is the area of the lower leg bone that lies just under the skin. This area has many nerves in it and causes a lot of pain when hit or scraped. The tibia (medical name for this bone) is very thick and difficult to break.

R. Instep:
The instep contains five of the bones in the foot known as the metatarsals. They are analogous to the bones on the back of the palm. The metatarsals are very thin and are easily broken. It is not uncommon for soldiers in the army to break one of these bones simply by marching too much. Fracture of these bones causes pain and difficulty standing on the affected foot.

BACK SIDE

A. Base of skull:
The base of the skull is where the spinal column attaches to the skull. The veins that drain blood from the brain also converge deep to this spot. A hard blow could break the spinal column causing paralysis or death or bleeding into the skull from tearing of these veins.

B. Outside elbow:
A blow to the outside or underneath the elbow can result in damage to the ligaments causing joint dislocation and inability to move the joint.

C. Inner wrist:
This is a favorite area for blocking punches because the arm bone in this region is not covered by protective muscles. A block to this area is painful and can produce a fracture.

D. Small of the back:
This area, also known as the lumbar region, overlays the kidneys. A blow to this area could tear the kidney causing blood loss or death. A hard blow could also tear the kidney loose from the back wall of the abdominal cavity causing it to fall into the pelvis.

E. Upper back:
This area, also known as the thoracic spine, is between the shoulder blades. It is less susceptible than the lower back to injury. A hard blow could fracture ribs as they attach to the vertebral column or fracture the vertebral column itself, causing paralysis.

F. Kidney:
Partially protected by the 12th rib so a strong blow is required; can produce kidney damage with associated severe pain.

G. Coccyx:
The coccyx refers to the very end of the spinal column. It is easily fractured because it is very thin. It is very painful when injured, causing inability to stand because of the pain.

H. Leg Joint:
Same as elbow; disrupts ligaments resulting in possible dislocation, pain and inability to bear weight.

I. Hollow of the knee:
This area (also called the popliteal fossa) contains the major blood vessels of the leg and very little protective muscle over them. A blow to this area could damage these vessels causing pain, bleeding and possibly gangrene of the leg from loss of blood supply.

J. Calves:
This area contains the muscles of the lower leg. A blow to this area could cause spasm of these muscles (a "charlie horse") and difficulty standing. Injury to the vessels in this area could cause bleeding.

K. Achilles' heel:
This is the nickname for the area where the tendon to the muscles of the calf attaches to the heel bone. This attachment is susceptible to injury when it is stepped on. The tendon is relatively easily torn away from the bone. This causes inability to stand on the affected leg because the muscles that attach are no longer able to hold the foot in the proper position required for standing. This is a very painful injury.

月の心

Tsuki no kokoro

"When facing your adversary, you must shine like the moon."

Japanese Maxim

CHAPTER THREE

Warm-up Exercises

Warm-up exercises 準備体操 are an integral part of any athletic activities and in karate training this also holds true. These exercises should be performed ten to fifteen minutes prior to each karate training session. Warm-ups are designed to increase muscle strength, limbering-up, endurance or wind and agility. Such action will gradually increase the heart rate, provide faster circulation to the working muscle, increase the body temperature and prepare the body to adapt to the overload. It will also assist the body in preventing joint and muscle injuries.

Another component of warm-up exercises is passive stretching, also called static stretching. This is done by slowly and gradually stretching the muscle while holding it at greater than resting length for a short time. In the leg stomach back-stretching (exercise 9), slowly raise both legs upward and overhead. Try to hold it for 10 seconds and recover by returning the legs to the starting position.

Since most of the body is used when executing karate techniques, it is advisable to start the exercises at the upper body and continue to the lower parts of the body.

Upon completion of karate training it is imperative to take the time to cool down. Cooling-down exercises will bring your body temperature back to a normal stage and help the muscles relax.

Shoulder-loosening (exercise 1)

- Stand with feet shoulder width apart, hands relaxed on each side.
- Raise the shoulders up and down (7 times).

Arm-stretching (exercise 2)

- Stand with feet shoulder width apart, hands relaxed at each side.
- Extend the right arm and rotate slowly in a backward circular motion (7 times).
- Repeat this procedure with the opposite hand.
- Extend both arms and rotate them faster in a backward circular motion (7 times).
- Repeat this procedure in a forward circular motion.

Hip-twisting (exercise 3)

- Stand and spread legs slightly more than shoulder width apart.
- Arms extended sideward at shoulder level.
- Twist hip to the left and then to the right side (7 times).

Knees-rotation (exercise 4)

- Stand naturally with feet together, knees slightly bent.
- Left hand grasping the left knee.
- Right hand grasping the right knee.
- Rotate both knees clockwise (7 times).
- Repeat this procedure in a counter-clockwise motion.

Leg and arm-stretching (exercise 5)

- While standing spread legs as far apart as possible.
- Keep knees straight.
- Bend upper body forward and right hand touches the left toes (7 times).
- Repeat this procedure with the opposite hand.

***Leg and arm-stretching with head touching the floor
(exercise 6)***

- Stand and spread legs as far apart as possible.
- Keep knees straight.
- Bend upper body forward and grab the left ankle with the left hand.
- Grab the right ankle with the right hand.
- Move the upper body forward and touch the floor with the forehead (7 times).

Leg-stretching (exercise 7)

- Sit on the floor with both legs spread as far apart as possible.
- Twist upper torso to the left.
- Grasp the left ankle with the left hand and touch the left knee with the forehead (7 times).
- Repeat this procedure on the opposite side.

Back-stretching (exercise 8)

- Sit on the floor with both legs together and extended forward.
- Both knees must be locked.
- Bend the upper body forward.
- Grab the left ankle with the left hand.
- Grab the right ankle with the right hand.
- Move the upper body forward and touch the knees with the forehead (7 times).

1

2

Leg stomach back-stretching (exercise 9)

- Lie flat on the back.
- Extend arms sideways approximately 45 degrees with palms touching the floor.
- Start exercise by raising both legs with heels 6 inches from the floor.
- Continue to raise the legs and swing both legs straight backward over the head until the toes touch the floor.
- Recover by returning the legs to the starting position (7 times).

1

2

Push-ups (exercise 10)

- Starting position is a front leaning rest position with fist clenched and hitting two knuckles on the floor, locking both elbows. Body straight from head to heels.
- Bend the elbows and lower chest approximately 4 inches from the floor.
- Raise the body and return to the starting position (7 times).

Sit-ups (exercise 11)

- Lie flat on the back with hands interlaced and placed on back of the head.
- Bend both knees with feet flat on the floor.
- Bend forward at the waist and raise the upper body until the elbow touches the knees (7 times).

Leg-stretching (Standing position) (exercise 12)

- Stand with feet shoulder width apart.
- Move right leg straight back approximately shoulder width apart.
- Front leg slightly bent.
- Kick right leg as high as possible directly in front of the body (7 times).
- Repeat this procedure with the opposite leg.

Leg-stretching (Standing position - clock and counterclockwise) (exercise 13)

- Stand with feet shoulder width apart.
- Move right leg straight back approximately shoulder width apart.
- Front leg slightly bent.
- Kick right leg as high as possible in a clockwise motion (7 times).
- Change to opposite stance.
- Kick left leg as high as possible in a counter-clockwise motion (7 times).

Knees-lifting (exercise 14)

- Stand with feet shoulder width apart.
- Move right leg straight back with front leg slightly bent.
- Slightly bend upper body.
- Raise right knee upward as high as possible and then lower to the floor (7 times).
- Repeat this procedure with the opposite knee.

Leg-stretching with a partner (exercise 15)

- Stand with feet shoulder width apart and hands relaxed on each side.
- Raise the right leg upward while the partner lifts the right foot as high as possible (1 time).
- Repeat this procedure with the opposite leg.
- Change position.
- Raise the right leg sideward while the partner lifts the right foot as high as possible (1 time).
- Repeat this procedure with the opposite leg.

CHAPTER FOUR

Stances and Maneuvers

Stances

The application of a strong defensive and offensive karate technique is largely contingent upon a stable stance スタンス or foundation. Karate-ka must be able to stand for minutes or longer in various positions and also be able to balance in many sequential movements. Japanese karate masters emphasized, "If the foundation is not sound, it would be unwise to continue building."

The following are essential requirements for a correct stance:

1. Concentration of power,

2. Eyes on the opponent,

3. Upper body upright with some exclusion,

4. Strong hips and

5. Correct Kokyu (Breathing).

Attention stance (Heisoku-dachi) 平足立ち

- Stand naturally with feet together.

Attention stance (feet turned outward) (Musubi-dachi) 結び立ち

- Stand naturally with heels together and feet pointed outward at a 45 degree angle.

Open stance (Hachiji-dachi) 八字立ち

- Stand naturally with feet shoulder width apart and fists clenched in front of the thighs.

Forward Stance (Zenkutsu-dachi) 前屈立ち

- Perform a stance with the left foot extended forward two shoulder widths apart.
- Bend front leg with knee over the big toe, keep upper body upright with rear leg straight.
- The total body weight is dispersed 60 percent on the front leg and 40 percent on the rear leg.

Riding horse stance (Kiba-dachi) 騎馬立ち

- Keep upper body upright.
- Spread feet two shoulder widths apart with toes slightly pointing inward.
- Bend knees and push firmly outward.
- Keep body weight equally dispersed on both legs.

Back stance (Kokutsu-dachi) 後屈立ち

- Keep upper body upright with feet two shoulder widths apart.
- Bend rear knee slightly forward and toes slightly inward.
- Keep knees outward.
- Front and back heel must be in a straight line. The total body weight is dispersed 30 percent on the front leg and 70 percent on the rear leg.

Cat stance (*Neko-ashi-dachi*) 猫足立ち

- Keep upper body upright.
- The back leg should be bent to support the entire body weight.
- The heel of the front leg should be raised lightly with the ball of the foot on the ground.

**Wide Hour glass stance
(Hangetsu-dachi)** 半月立ち

- Perform a combination of two stances; forward modified stance with left foot extended forward and hour glass stance.
- Keep upper body upright.
- Both knees should be slightly bent inward.
- Tense lower abdomen.

Hour glass stance (Sanchin-dachi) 三戦立ち

- Keep upper body upright.
- Both knees should be slightly bent inward.
- Distance between feet should be 18 inches.
- The front heel and rear toes are in line with each other.
- Keep body weight equally dispersed on both feet.
- Tense lower abdomen.

Immovable stance (Fudou-Dachi) 不動立ち

- Perform a combination of two stances; forward stance with left foot extended forward and horse riding stance (two shoulder widths apart).
- The front knee is over the left big toe.
- The right knee is approximately one foot forward of the right big toe.
- Total body weight is equally dispersed between both legs, with knees bent and outward tension.

Maneuvers

There are various types of maneuvers サバキ in karate such as: Upper body deflecting, stepping, turning and sliding. When executing the various types of maneuvers the karate-ka must maintain strong posture and balance.

With constant practice and knowledge of these techniques the practitioner's maneuver will be undetected by the opponent.

Upper body deflecting (Jotai Sabaki) 上体サバキ

- Assume fighting stance.
- Left hand deflects punch away from the face.
- Right fist is clenched in a ready position.

45

Stepping forward (Zenkutsu-Dachi De Zenshin) 前屈立ちで前進

- Assume forward stance with the left leg forward.
- The front leg pulls and pushes the body forward.
- Simultaneously, the right foot lightly sweeps the ground and the right leg guards the lower vital area.

Stepping forward in a back stance (Kokutsu-Dachi De Zenshin)
後屈立ちで前進

- Assume back stance with the left leg forward.
- When moving forward, lightly sweep the ground with the right foot by pivoting on the left foot in one fluid motion.

***Riding horse stance side stepping** (Kiba-Dachi De Saido Suttepu)*
騎馬立ちでサイドステップ

- Assume riding horse stance.
- Move by crossing the right foot over and next to the left foot.
- Continue the lateral motion by assuming the riding horse stance.

48

Turn around in a forward stance (Zenkutsu-Dachi De Kaiten)
前屈立ちで回転

- Assume forward stance with the left leg forward.
- Sweep the right foot laterally to the left one and one-half shoulder widths. Pivot on the balls of the feet to face the opposite direction.

***Forward stance sliding to a front kick position (Zenkutsu-Dachi
Kara Mae Geri No Shisei)*** 前屈立ちから前蹴りのポジション

- Assume forward stance with the left leg forward.
- Slide the right rear foot in place of the front left foot and
  simultaneously raise the front leg to chest level.

CHAPTER FIVE

Punching and Striking Techniques

Punching Techniques

In chapter one, I have stated that the word Karate-Do means "empty-handed way." One of the natural weapons of the empty-handed practitioner is the punch. The punch can be used to subdue the armed or unarmed attacker. A punching technique 手技 can be fully developed only by understanding that the practitioner must maintain a stable stance. In addition, the karate-ka must have the correct understanding of how to generate power by maximizing the use of the legs and hips.

In our daily chores we use our hands for various reasons such as: combing our hair, washing our face, brushing our teeth, putting on and removing our clothes and many other tasks. This is also valid in karate where there is a tendency to use more hand than leg techniques. However, one should strive to equalize the two.

The three types of punching techniques will be illustrated on the following pages:

1. Fore fist straight punch,

2. Lunge punch and

3. Reverse punch.

Fore fist straight punch (*Seiken-choku-zuki*) 正拳突き

- Assume an open stance.
- Extend the left arm forward with the palm facing downward.
- Cock the right arm with the palm facing upward approximately one inch above the belt.
- Keep right fist close to the ribs.
- Make certain to pull the elbow inward.
- Punch in a straight line, brushing the elbow lightly along the ribs and simultaneously retract the left arm brushing the elbow lightly along the ribs (as if hitting an opponent behind with the elbow).
- At the moment of impact, twist both wrists simultaneously and focus (kime).
- Only the knuckles of the index and middle finger should strike the target.
- The punching arm should be slightly bent.

Lunge punch (Oi-zuki) 追い突き

- Refer to the fore fist straight punch.
- Assume forward stance with the left leg forward.
- Extend left arm and cock the right hand on the right hip.
- Left leg pulls and pushes the body forward as you simultaneously punch with the right hand in a straight line.
- As you move forward the right foot lightly sweeps the ground and the right leg guards the lower vital area.
- Hips must be inward and body upright.

Reverse punch (Gyaku-zuki) 逆突き

- Assume forward stance with the left leg forward.
- The punching fist is on the opposite side of the front leg.
- Initial move of the reverse punch is turning the hips inward followed by the punching arm.
- Simultaneously, retract the left hand against the left hip.
- At the moment of impact, lock the rear leg and focus (kime).
- Keep the upper body upright and make certain the punching hand's elbow brushes lightly along the ribs.
- When retracting the punching hand, do not move the front leg (only the hips and the rear leg should move).

Striking Techniques

Striking with the hand involves more of a semicircular snapping motion using the elbow as a fulcrum.

One must understand that these striking techniques 打ち技 can also be used in defensive situations.

Elbow strike (Empi-uchi) 猿臂打ち

- Use to strike face, armpit, floating ribs or solar plexus.
- Assume forward stance with the right leg forward.
- Extend right hand with the palm facing downward and the left fist against right rib.
- Move left leg forward into riding horse stance and strike the opponent with the left elbow.
- Simultaneously retract the right fist against the right rib.
- Elbow strike can be used upward, forward, backward or sideward.

Back fist strike (Uraken-uchi) 裏拳打ち

- Use to strike face, floating ribs or solar plexus.
- Assume forward stance with the right leg forward.
- Strike with the right hand in a curve like motion and in an upright direction.
- Simultaneously retract the left fist against the left rib.
- Make sure both fists are tightly clenched.
- Hit the target by utilizing the surface of the first two knuckles of the fist.

Knife hand strike (Shuto-uchi) 手刀打ち

- Use to strike temple, neck or floating ribs.
- Assume forward stance with the left leg forward.
- Extend left opened hand palm facing downward.
- Move right leg forward with right opened hand on right ear and elbow almost level with the ear.
- Strike with the right hand in a wide curve motion utilizing the arm's rotation.
- Keep the palm facing upward.
- Simultaneously retract the left fist against the left rib.

Palm heel strike (Teisho-uchi) 掌底打ち

- Use to strike temple, chin, solar plexus, floating ribs or groin.
- Assume forward stance with the left leg forward.
- Extend left palm heel hand straight upward approximately 120 degrees at chin level with the right fist against right ribs.
- Move right leg forward while retracting the left hand half way to chest level and then strike with the right palm heel.
- Simultaneously retract the left fist against the left ribs.
- In practice, this should be one fluid motion.

CHAPTER SIX

Blocking Techniques

The title, <u>KARATE-DO: The Art of Defense</u>, emphasizes that karate is not an offensive but a defensive art. For this reason it is to the practitioner's advantage to train and develop blocking techniques 受け技 to the fullest extent. The initial movement in karate is always a blocking movement followed by a counter attack. Karate masters always stress this teaching to their practitioners "never to attack first." However, defensive and offensive movements can be executed to cause the same results. For example, the opponent attacks with a lunge punch to the lower part of the defender's body. The defender blocks the attack so forcefully resulting in severe pain to the opponent thus, deterring any further attack.

The following points should be considered when blocking:

1. Unbalance your opponent's attack with your block.

2. Remember to be relaxed, not standing like a statue and concentrate your focus with the incoming attack.

3. Turn your hip quickly and forcefully to the side at a 45 degree angle. This reduces the target area exposed to your opponent's attack and puts you in a position to execute a reverse punch counter attack.

4. If the opportunity arises, attack your opponent before he begins his attack (Sen-No-Sen).

Upper block (Jodan-uke) 上げ受け

- Use to block an attack to the upper level.
- Assume forward stance with the left leg forward.
- Bend left arm in front of the forehead and move forward while raising the right arm.
- As the right arm passes in front of the body, twist inward (a feeling that you are hitting a target).
- Turn the body facing half way away from the opponent as you block.
- Focus at the point one fist distance between the forehead and fist.
- Right thumb is facing downward and left arm is in the cocked position against the left ribs.

Downward block (Gedan-barai) 下段払い

- Use to block an attack to the lower level area.
- Assume forward stance with the left leg forward and the left hand one fist distance from the knee.
- Right fist against the right ribs.
- Move forward extending the left arm and move right fist to the left ear (block with a feeling of slicing an object).
- Turn the body facing half way away from the opponent as you block.
- Focus the block above the knee at one fist distance between the wrist and knee.
- Simultaneously retract left fist against the left ribs.
- Do not forget to twist the wrist at the moment you block the opponent's arm or leg.

Knife hand block (Shuto-uke) 手刀受け

- Use to block an attack to the middle level area.
- Assume back stance with the left leg forward.
- Extend left open hand palm facing downward and move forward with right hand on the left ear.
- Continue by slicing forearm downward in a diagonal motion.
- Twist blocking arm inward upon contact.
- Retract left hand palm facing upward in front of the solar plexus.
- Right hand elbow should be bent at an angle of 90 degrees (protecting rib area).
- Keep one fist distance between elbow and ribs.

Forearm block

A. Outside block (Soto ude-uke) 外受け

- Use to block an attack to the middle level area.
- Assume forward stance with the left leg forward; extend left hand half way.
- Have a feeling of grabbing an opponent's hand.
- Move forward with the right elbow bent and the right fist behind the right ear.
- Continue by swinging right forearm in front of the body.
- Left hand retracts to left ribs.
- Turn the wrist upon contact.
- Turn the body facing half way away from the opponent as you block.
- Make certain the elbow is bent at an angle of 90 degrees (protecting rib area).

B. Inside block (Uchi-uke) 内受け

- Same stance as the outside forearm block; extend left hand straight forward.
- Have a feeling of grabbing the opponent's hand.
- Move forward with the right arm bent and right fist under the left armpit.
- Swing and block right forearm in front of the body.
- Simultaneously retract left fist against the ribs.
- Keep elbow bent at an angle of 90 degrees.

Double forearm block (Morote-uke) 諸手受け

- Use to block an attack to the middle level area.
- Assume forward stance with the left leg forward.
- Keep left arm bent 90 degrees in front of the body with the little finger of the right fist barely touching the left elbow.
- Move forward swinging both arms with the fists pointing down close to the left hip.
- Simultaneously pull the right leg forward.
- Swing both arms sharply so the right arm is bent 90 degrees in front of the body and the left fist's little finger barely touches the right elbow.

X-block (Juji-uke) 十字受け

- Use to block an attack to the upper and lower level areas.
- Assume an open stance, clench fists in front of the thighs.
- Raise both fists to the right side of the chest, right fist should be slightly on top of the left wrist.
- Move left leg forward and simultaneously thrust both hands downward.
- Keep upper body in a vertical position.
- Always remember to…? Focus.

Crescent-kick block (*Mikazuki-geri*) 三日月蹴り

- Use to block an attack to the middle level area.
- Assume forward stance with the left leg forward.
- Raise right foot and swing in an arc like motion in front of the body.
- Strike with the sole of the kicking foot.
- Simultaneously the upper body moves in conjunction with the supporting pivot leg.

空手の練習時、腕と足
は刀のようと思うべし

*"When you practice karate, think of your
arms and legs as swords."*

Azato

CHAPTER SEVEN

Leg Techniques

S ince the human leg is very powerful, it is not exaggerating to state that leg techniques 足技 can be developed to be a very devastating force.

The following are essential requirements for correct leg techniques:

1. Concentration of power,

2. Raise the knee of kicking leg to chest level,

3. Maintain a stable supported leg - foot cemented on the ground and knee slightly bent,

4. Withdraw the kicking leg double the speed of the initial kick and

5. Utilization of the hips.

For the majority of kicking techniques, withdraw the kicking leg double the speed of the initial kick to the front of the body and return to the previous stance (roundhouse kick is the exception).

Front kick

- This can be executed from forward stance with the left leg forward.
- Raise the right knee to chest level and curl the toes.
- Kick to the front of the body by utilizing the hips to push the ankle in a forward motion.
- At the moment of impact always remember to focus.
- Withdraw.

A. Front snap kick (Maegeri-keage) 前蹴り 蹴上げ

- Assume the same stance and body positioning as front kick.
- Utilize the snapping movement of the kicking knee.
- Strike the target with the ball of the kicking foot.
- Withdraw.

B. Front thrust kick (Maegeri-kekomi) 前蹴り蹴込み

- Assume the same stance and body positioning as front kick.
- Thrust your foot straight to the target (Utilization of your hips is more pronounced in this kick).
- Strike the target with the ball or heel of the kicking foot.
- Withdraw.

Side Kick

- This can be executed from forward, riding horse or any other stance.
- Utilize the edge or heel of the striking foot.
- Withdraw.

A. Side snap kick (Yoko-geri-keage) 横蹴り蹴上げ

- Raise the kicking foot.
- Kick by utilizing the snapping movement of the knee.
- Withdraw.

B. Side thrust kick (Yoko-geri-kekomi) 横蹴り蹴込み

- Raise the kicking foot above the supporting knee and thrust the movement of the kick.
- Withdraw.

Back kick (Ushiro-geri) 後ろ蹴り

- Assume forward stance with the left leg forward.
- Raise the right knee to chest level and bend stationary leg.
- Look to the rear and strike the target with the heel thrusting the kicking leg in a straight line.
- Withdraw.

Roundhouse kick (Mawashi-geri) 回し蹴り

- Assume forward stance with the left leg forward.
- Raise the right leg and keep it horizontal to the ground with the heel pulled back.
- A snapping movement of the kicking knee and rotating of the hips are performed in unison.
- Strike the target with the ball of the kicking foot.
- Withdraw the kicking leg double the speed of the initial kick, keeping it horizontal to the ground and returning to the previous stance.

Knee kick (Hittsui-geri) 膝蹴り

- Assume forward stance with the left leg forward.
- Lunge both hands to the opponent's head, grab and draw his head downward and simultaneously raise the right knee striking the opponent's face.

Spinning heel kick (Kaiten Ushiro-Geri) 回転後ろ蹴り

- Assume forward stance with the left leg forward.
- Keep eyes fixed on the target.
- Move by utilizing the left pivot foot and rotating the body 180 degrees to the right.
- Keep eyes constantly fixed on the target.
- Right leg continues to travel in a circular movement striking the target with the heel.

明日の勝利は今日の練習から

"Tomorrow's victory is won after today's practice."

Samurai Maxim

CHAPTER EIGHT

Training Program

In order to manage karate training time effectively, I have designed different types of training programs 練習プログラム to benefit the karate-ka.

This chapter deals with the following training programs:

A. Suggested dojo training.

B. Suggested outside dojo training.

C. Flow chart of karate-do progress training.

D. Training equipment.

E. Suggested combinations.

F. Advancement to higher degrees.

A. Suggested Dojo Training

A common training schedule is Tuesday, Thursday and Saturday for a period of two hours each training day.

<u>Tuesday</u>

Basics

Combinations

Kicks

Three and five step sparring

Total of fifteen kata

Straw-padded post punching prior to each training

One step sparring

One step realistic sparring

Free sparring

<u>Thursday</u>

Same as Tuesday

<u>Saturday</u>

Same as Tuesday with heavy emphasis upon kata training

Total of twenty-four kata

B. Suggested Outside Dojo Training

A common training schedule is Monday, Wednesday and Friday for a period of one hour each training day.

Monday

Total of twelve kata

Straw-padded post punching

Bag Kicking

Front kick

Side kick

Roundhouse kick

Back kick

Spinning heel kick

Flying kick

Wednesday

Same as Monday

Friday

Kata training only. Total of twenty-four kata.

C. Flow Chart of Karate–Do Progress Training

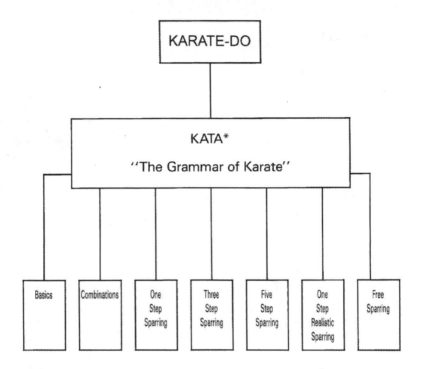

空手道

KARATE-DO

KATA*

"The Grammar of Karate"

| Basics | Combinations | One Step Sparring | Three Step Sparring | Five Step Sparring | One Step Realistic Sparring | Free Sparring |

*Chapter Nine – Kata and Kumite

D. Training Equipment

1. Training uniform or "Gi"

The training uniform or Gi consists of a shirt, pants and a belt. White color of shirt and pants is suggested over the black Gi. Gi's that are made of light or medium material which allow the body to move freely are more acceptable. There are different types of belts and color variations according to the specific styles of karate. The color of belts widely used are white, yellow, green, purple, blue, brown and black.

Training Uniform

Karate Uniform Sizing Chart

Size	Height	Weight	
00	4'4"	60 lbs.	Children's size
0	4'6"	85	Children's size
1	4'9"	105 (or less)	Adult size
2	4'10"-5'3"	106-120	
3	5'4"-5'6"	121-135	
4	5'7"-5'9"	136-165	
5	5'10"-6'	166-200	
6	6'1" and up	201 (or over)	Extra large

2. Straw-padded post

The length of the post is approximately 7 feet, 3½ inches in width and placed about 3 feet firmly into the ground. The total length of the straw pad is one foot, 2½ inches in thickness and 3½ inches in width. The straw bundle is tightly tied with the straw rope. Place the straw pad on the post and tie it securely with two ropes approximately one inch from the top and bottom end.

What are the benefits?

1. Improves the maximum application of focus at the moment of impact.

2. Straw-padded post training is the best method to improve stronger punching and striking techniques.

3. Straw-padded post training enables one to increase the threshold of human pain.

4. Improves punching accuracy with the two knuckles hitting the target and strengthening of the wrist.

The following punching and striking methods are always beneficial to train:

1. Riding horse stance punch.

2. Forward stepping lunge punch.

3. Forward stance reverse punch.

4. Knife hand strike.

5. Back hand strike.

6. Back fist strike.

7. Bottom fist strike.

8. Elbow strike.

9. Palm heel strike.

10. Hook punch.

Forward stance reverse punch

Knife hand strike

Elbow strike

86

3. Kicking bag

Hang the kicking bag by hooking the handle to a swivel hook attached to the ceiling. The bag's bottom needs to be at the height of your abdomen.

What are the benefits?

1. Improves balancing.

2. Improves strengthening of leg muscles.

3. Improves timing.

4. Improves hip action.

5. Improves focusing.

The following foot techniques are always beneficial to train:

1. Front kick.

2. Side kick.

3. Roundhouse kick.

4. Back kick.

5. Spinning heel kick.

6. Flying front kick.

7. Flying side kick.

8. Crescent kick.

9. Stamping kick.

10. Knee kick.

Practicing roundhouse kick

Practicing spinning heel kick

4. Pulleys

Fasten two pulleys to the ceiling approximately 3 feet apart and insert a rope through the pulleys that will allow both ends to touch the ground. One end of the rope has a canvas loop tied on the rope to hook the foot.

What are the benefits?

1. Improves limbering of leg muscles.

2. Improves kicking techniques.

Stretching front leg

Stretching side leg

5. Mirror

Utilize in detecting "telegraphing movements" and improving all of the karate techniques such as blocking, punching, striking and kicking. Telegraphing movements are premovements or hesitations which alert the opponent to your intentions. For example, a gritting of the teeth prior to a lunge punch is a "telegraphing movement."

Detecting "telegraphing movements"

6. Protective gear

It is an ideal piece of equipment for practicing punching and kicking techniques. However, keep in mind that the gear is <u>not</u> an insurance against injury. Do not fully exert your punching/kicking force. Also, it can be used as protective gear during sparring.

Practicing lunge punch

E. Suggested Combinations

Perform in forward stance (followed by reverse punches).

1. Upper block then execute reverse punch to the face or solar plexus.

2. Downward block then execute reverse punch to the face or solar plexus.

3. Forearm block then execute reverse punch to the face or solar plexus.

4. Lunge punch to the face then execute reverse punch to the solar plexus.

5. Front kick (rl) to the stomach then execute reverse punch to the face.

Upper block then execute reverse punch to the face or solar plexus.

Kicking

Perform from any stance.

1. Front kick (rl) to the solar plexus then execute side kick (sl) to the face.

2. Side kick (rl) to the face then execute front kick (ol) to the solar plexus.

3. Front kick (rl) to the solar plexus, side kick (ol) to the face then execute back kick (initial kicking leg) to the solar plexus.

4. Roundhouse kick (rl) to the face then execute front kick (ol) to the solar plexus.

5. Front kick (rl) to the solar plexus then execute roundhouse kick (ol) to the face.

6. Front kick (fl) with the same leg twice to the face or solar plexus.

Roundhouse kick (rl) to the solar plexus then execute back fist to the face.

1

2

   Crescent kick (rl) then execute side kick (sl) to the solar plexus.

Other Combinations

Main targets are face and solar plexus.

1. Side kick (rl), roundhouse kick (ol) then execute reverse punch.

2. Reverse punch, front kick (rl) then execute reverse punch.

3. Two roundhouse kicks (fl) only.

4. Two front kicks (rl) only.

5. Crescent kick (rl) then execute back kick with the same leg.

6. Front kick (rl) then execute jumping front kick (ol).

7. Roundhouse kick (rl) then execute right backfist strike to the face, then reverse punch with left fist.

(rl) - rear leg

(ol) - other leg

(sl) - same leg

(fl) - front leg

F. Advancement to Higher Degrees

Degrees/Belts	Requirements for Advancement
1st Dan Black	Written test...Basics...Combinations Five Heian...Three Tekki...Advanced Kata...3 step...5 step...Breaking... 1 step...Kata applications...Sparring
1st Kyu Brown/three strip	Written test...Basics...Combinations...
2nd Kyu Brown/two strip	Five Heian...Three Tekki...3 step...
3rd Kyu Brown/one strip	5 step...Breaking...1 step... Kata applications...Sparring
4th Kyu Blue	Written test...Basics...Combinations... Five Heian...One Tekki...3 step... 5 step...Breaking...1 step... Kata applications...Sparring
5th Kyu Purple	Written test...Basics...Combinations... Five Heian...3 step...5 step... Breaking...1 step... Kata applications...Sparring
6th Kyu Green	Written test...Basics...Combinations... Three Heian...3 step...5 step... Breaking...1 step...Kata applications
7th Kyu Yellow	Written test...Basics...One Heian... 3 step...5 step,..1 step... Kata applications
8th Kyu White/one strip	Basics
9th Kyu White	Basics

Testing occurs four times a year (March, June, September and December).The testing committee will administer the testing degrees and Dan/Kyu.

CHAPTER NINE

Kata and Kumite

Kata

What is kata 型? To the onlooker it might seem like an acrobatic act, dancing routine or shadow boxing exercise. For the karate-ka the Japanese word kata or forms is a series of pre-arranged karate techniques of defensive and offensive movements without the presence of one or more opponents. Kata consists of all the different types of karate basic movements such as blocking, punching, striking, kicking, body maneuvering, balance and throwing techniques. All kata of karate begin with one or more defensive movements thus revealing the non-violence of the art.

The stomach (hara), is the point three inches below the navel and the storage area of the ki 氣. It has an important function, to act as the governor of the whole body during the execution phase of the kata. When executing the kata, make a point that all the joints will move simultaneously. When one part moves, all other parts move.

Through continuous practice and with understanding the karate-ka will come to appreciate kata. Mastering kata requires serious study and hard training.

Many centuries ago prominent karate masters created these kata and refined them to their standards. Some of the current kata that the present karate-ka is learning were actually "tested in real combat situations." Karate masters have handed down twenty to fifty kata which are actively being practiced by many karate-ka throughout the world. Japanese masters considered kata the "spirit of karate." Kata are classified into two original dominant groups:

I. Shorei school (Naha-te) - emphasis upon flexibility and strength.

Kata from the Shorei school are:

Tekki I thru III (Horse riding)

Jitte (Ten hands)

Hangetsu (Crescent or half moon)

Jion (Name of the founder)

II. Shorin school (Shuri-te) - emphasis upon speed and readiness.

Kata from the Shorin school are:

Taikyoku I through III (First cause)

Heian I thru V (Peaceful mind)

Bassai-Dai (To penetrate a fortress)

Kanku-Dai (Sky viewing)

Empi (Flying swallow)

Gankaku (Crane on a rock)

III. Other kata are:

Chinte (Extraordinary hands)   Meikyo (Mirror of the Soul)

Bassai-Sho (The lesser Bassai)   Wankan (King's crown)

Sochin (Tranquil Force)   Jiin (Temple grounds)

Kanku-Sho (The lesser Kanku) Gojushiho Dai (Fifty-four steps)

Unsu (Hands in the clouds)   Gojushiho Sho (The lesser Gojushiho)

Nijushiho (Twenty-four steps)

Master Hidehiko (Hidy) Ochiai, a noted teacher of Washin Ryu Karate-Do, stated, "He considers kata to be the grammar of karate. If a person does not learn the proper grammar of a language first, he will speak poorly. The same principle applies to karate. Without learning the basic forms that develop balance, speed and power, a person will perform karate poorly."[3] Many trophies have been won by Hidy's students who have based their training upon this simple principle.

What is the proper method of learning kata?

1. Learn the individual movements.

2. Understand the meaning of the individual movements.

3. Strive toward the goal of quality as opposed to the quantity learned.

---

[3] *From* OFFICIAL KARATE: Personal Profile: Hidehiko (Hidy) Ochiai Spiritual Warrior. *Copyright (c) 1974 by Charlton Publications, Inc., Derby, Conn.*

Why do karate masters highly stress continual kata training? The reason is to develop:

1. Sensing ability

2. Breathing and ki flow

3. Coordination

4. Posture

5. Balance

6. Speed

7. Maximum application of power or "kime"

8. Rhythm

9. Timing

10. Maneuvers

Application of Heian Nidan

1

2

Application of Heian Nidan

Kumite

The word kumite 組手 means to engage (Kumi) with hand or hands (Te). It is an actual combat situation between two practitioners utilizing the application of kata techniques. There are five different types of kumite:

1. One step sparring 基本組手

2. Three step sparring 三本組手

3. Five step sparring 五本組手

4. One step realistic sparring 自由一本組手

5. Free sparring 自由組手

One step sparring: One attacks the opponent in a predetermined target area one time (to the upper, middle or lower section of the body). The opponent blocks a single attack and counters.

1

2

3

4

Three step sparring: One attacks the opponent in a predetermined target area three times starting with the right fist (to the upper, middle or lower section of the body). The opponent defends himself. After the third attack, the defender counter attacks with his fist and K.O.'s the attacker. Accompanied with a yell Kiai "feeling together."

1

2

107

3

4

5

6 <u>**Five step sparring**</u>: One attacks the opponent in a predetermined target area five times starting with the right fist (to the upper, middle or lower section of the body). The opponent defends himself. After the fifth attack, the defender counter attacks with his fist and K.O.'s the attacker. Accompanied with a yell "Kiai." Three and five step sparring will enable the karate-ka to improve the speed of his forward and backward maneuvers.

1

2

One step realistic sparring: The attacker and defender agree upon a predetermined target area and how the attack will be executed. Both partners bow to each other, assume their fighting positions and are free to move as they desire. The attacker has to cause an opening and the defender has to be on guard at all times. Once the attacker executes his attack, the defender blocks and then counter attacks applying kata techniques.

1

2

3

Free sparring: The opponent's attacks are no longer predetermined.

In 1935, a Japanese karate master called "The Cat," Gogen Yamaguchi, developed free sparring in which the practitioners trained against each other and utilized kata techniques. Free sparring is similar to a boxing match except that these attacks must be controlled to prevent bodily injuries to either practitioner. Both practitioners must assume relaxed, ready positions to attack or defend at any given moment. This type of kumite must be practiced only by advanced practitioners having learned the fundamentals and strong karate techniques.

Free sparring training will improve the practitioner's:

1. Timing ability,

2. Quick movement,

3. Ability to detect the opponent's tactics or attacks,

4. Ability to detect one's shortcomings and

5. A sense of combativeness.

1

2

113

3

4

Free sparring against the opponent's roundhouse kick.

1

2

3

Free sparring one against two opponents

戦無抑制は、百戦全勝より上

"For, to win one hundred victories in one hundred battles is not the highest skill. To subdue the enemy without fighting is the highest skill."[4]

---

[4] *From <u>The Karate-Do Kyohan: The Master Text</u> by Gichin Funakoshi. Copyright and published by Kodansha International Ltd., 1973. Tokyo, p. 248*

CHAPTER TEN

Nutrition Produces Performance

The wise karate practitioner should know that nutrition is the best preventive medicine of today and will be more so in the future.

Proper nutrition and supplementation may help avoid a host of ills; including broken bones, weight loss, fatigue, muscular sprains and others, which due to the increased level of accelerated activity, are more prevalent to the karate-ka.

The foundation of any good nutritional program is a natural vitamin and mineral supplement in sufficient levels to actually strengthen the brain, muscles, nerves, bones, blood (cardiovascular system) and immune system.

A common misconception heard often these days is that you can get all the nutrition you need by eating a balanced diet. The so-called "balanced diet" consists of food chosen daily from the four basic food groups: Meat - Protein, Grain - Carbohydrate, Milk and Dairy Products and Fruits/Vegetables.

It is good to eat food daily from the four basic food groups, however, it is known today that athletes have specific nutritional needs based upon their particular activity.

Also, it has been stated that most Americans don't eat a balanced diet; even those few who do still need supplementation for several reasons:

1. The soil in most areas has been so depleted due to ignoring God's Laws for its use and overuse of chemical fertilizers that the food produced is often lacking in proper vitamin and mineral content.

2. Recent information indicates that you would have to eat such large quantities of certain foods that pesticide poisoning would be a real concern (there are over ninety pesticides that can legally be used to treat an apple).

Fresh fruit and vegetables are best if organically grown (no pesticides or chemical fertilizers). In lieu of that, a 30 minute soaking in lemon juice (I TBS), cider vinegar (1 TBS) and purified water (1 quart) helps to remove pesticides.

The following is an interview between A.O. Mercado, author and karate instructor, and Donald R. Hendrickson, owner, HEARTLAND HEALTH FOODS, 6000-F Leavenworth Road, Kansas City, Kansas 66104.

"Don, I've read about Vitamin C and its many benefits. Could you tell me how Vitamin C and a few other specific vitamins could be helpful to the karate-ka?"

"That's a good question, A.O. Fresh citrus fruits such as oranges, lemons, limes and grapefruit, contain this vitamin (approximately 70 mg. Vitamin C per orange). Vitamin C helps accelerate healing, builds muscle tissue, fine bones and teeth, prevents colds and flu, decreases blood cholesterol (blood fats), prevents viral infections, stimulates the immune system, heals scars, wounds, gums, heart and damaged body tissue, decreases allergies and reduces anxiety. Vitamin C reduces blood clots, thereby, preventing heart attacks. It has also been proven to prevent rancidity in cells. Large doses of C have been used successfully to treat cancer patients and drug addicts. It builds collagen (skin connective tissue), which retards aging. C lubricates the fluid of joints (synovial fluid) allowing freer, easier movement which should be especially helpful to the karate-ka. 250 mg. per 40 pounds of body weight is a good guideline for Vitamin C dosage.

Also C is better absorbed if taken with bioflavonoids (usually derived from lemons). Bioflavonoids build up the walls of the cardiovascular system and help to prevent strokes, varicose veins, hemorrhaging, etc.

Vitamin E is another vitamin the karate-ka should consider. Look for D-Alpha Tocopherol Vitamin E. It's the natural E and has been proven to be utilized by the body better than synthetic. 400 to 800 I.U. of E a day will give the karate-ka more endurance and stamina as it increases the oxygen supply to body tissues and lungs, it alleviates fatigue, retards aging, accelerates healing, prevents and dissolves blood clots, thereby protecting the heart, relieves cramps, helps to heal without scarring when applied to the skin and taken internally. E is important to male sexual health and stamina along with Zinc. In females, 400 to 1200 I.U. (International Units) relieves PMS (pre-menstrual syndrome), hot flashes and promotes fertility in males and females. Some natural E sources are wheat germ, soybeans, whole wheat, grain cereals, eggs and leafy greens. There are many fine natural E supplements such as Dry E, Selenium and Lecithin all in one capsule. Dry Vitamin E is suggested if high blood pressure is present or for people who can't tolerate oils. Excessive yawning, dry skin and fatigue can be a sign of Vitamin E and C deficiency because of lack of oxygen to the cells."

"Don, drawing upon your years of experience in the health and nutritional field, could you tell me what are some suggestions to nutritionally prevent broken bones?"

"A.O., the dietary way to build strong bones and teeth is to drink several glasses of milk a day and eat several ounces of cheese or dairy products. Since many of us don't do this daily, the experts advise that it is wise to supplement with at least 1000 mg. of calcium and 500 mg. of magnesium daily. (If one tends toward broken bones, this can be increased to 1500 mg. of calcium and 750 mg. of magnesium daily). Make sure the supplement you use is approximately 2 to 1, Calcium to Magnesium or equal in Cal-Mag. The magnesium is essential for proper calcium absorption. It not only helps to prevent kidney stones, it helps to build strong nerves. Studies have proven that calcium is better absorbed by the body while we sleep; magnesium is a natural relaxer, so take your Cal-Mag supplement at bedtime. There are several herbs that build strong bones, muscles, tendons and ligaments. Horsetail silica herb builds strong bones and connective tissue. Comfrey is called the "boneknitter" herb, because it helps broken bones to heal quickly and strengthens the bones. These can be taken separately or there are some good combinations on the market. This blend is also great to protect against muscular sprains. If you do get a sprain, it is advisable to apply ice immediately to avoid swelling. After that - rest. DMSO (dimethyl sulfoxide) comes in creams, liquids, gels and applied to the skin, it relieves pain and swelling immediately. DMSO is used safely by many professional athletes."

"Don, I drink purified water. How important is the type of water we drink and how much should we drink and eat before competition?"

"Well, A.O., because our bodies are two-thirds water, the lack of water is the most frequent deciding factor between winning and losing in any athletic competition, especially a strenuous activity such as karate. A good rule to go by is to drink 8 ounces of water (preferably purified or distilled) for each 49 pounds of body weight before you begin competition. Then drink 8 ounces for each 14 min. of physical activity.

Eat at least two hours before competition or training. If the karate-ka is extremely nervous prior to competition, he may want to eat three to four hours prior to the event and don't eat big. Complex carbohydrates, whole grain breads and cereals, whole grains, fruits, pasta, vegetables, brown rice (¼ to ½ cup), fresh fruit, orange juice and skimmed or low fat milk; these are some of the recommended foods. Oils and fats should be kept to a minimum as they slow down the emptying of the stomach and the release of needed energy nutrients. Supplements should be taken two hours prior to competition. After competition, drink 8 ounces for each 49 pounds of body weight beyond thirst to replace much needed body water. Also, a good liquid supplement to replace electrolytes (water soluble minerals) before or after competition is trace mineral liquid or tabs, (available in most health food stores)."

"You've said supplements should be taken two hours prior to competition. Could you tell us more about that?"

"Yes. Ginseng is used by many athletes to increase stamina, performance and productivity and justifiably so.

Sir Edwin Arnold, a noted Orientalist, stated, 'According to the Chinese, Asiatic Ginseng is the best and most potent of all cordials, stimulants, tonics, cardiacs, and above all, will best renovate and reinvigorate falling forces. It fills the heart with hilarity while its occasional use will, it is said, add a decade to human life. Have all these millions of Orientals, all these many generations of men who boiled ginseng in silver kettles and praised heaven for its many benefits been totally deceived?'

'No! Modern clinical research supports Ginseng. It is an adaptogen herb or body normalizer going to where it's needed in the body and doing its wonderful work. Ginseng has been proven in a long term study to build a resistance to stress; it also increases vitality, endurance, invigorates the immune system, improves brain and muscle function, overall health, relieves depression and anxiety and increases sexual vitality even into old age. It is a gentle stimulant, raising or lowering blood pressure as needed in individual cases. It's no wonder that the Chinese call it 'man root.' Ginseng is mentioned in the Bible in Ezekiel 27:17. 'Pannag', referring to Panax which means 'panacea' or 'it works on any problem.'

Bee Pollen is called 'Nature's only perfect food', rich in ninety-seven discernable nutrients. Many athletes use Bee Pollen for increased energy, endurance and stamina. A high desert American bee pollen in granulated form or in capsules is very pure and effective.

Another supplement widely used by athletes for staying power is Octacosanol, a derivative from the heart of wheat germ. You'll hear more about this and other super supplements as studies are being done which validate their effectiveness. The great thing about these natural power boosters is that they may be used together and they are totally beneficial to improve overall health and endurance."

"A.O., I'd like to add the following under the supplement section. We also market an excellent energy complex under our own label, HEARTLAND HEALTH FOODS, that is safe, effective and can help to improve mental clarity and memory as well; it is called Guarana Complex 1000 mg., and could be taken at least two hours before karate competition to naturally improve reflexes, performance and endurance. In South America they also believe that Guarana helps to prevent many diseases."

"As you know, Don, the karate-ka loses weight rapidly during practice or competition. What are some effective ways to gain this weight back that's being lost?"

"While we're on this subject, A.O., I'd like to advise that never should anyone use steroids to gain weight or muscle. Their benefits are short term and the detriments, such as unbalancing the body chemistry and liver cancer, can kill the steroid user.

There are several safe, natural ways to gain weight and muscle. The diet should be well balanced consisting of whole, unrefined foods. High calorie foods such as seeds, nuts, butter, salad oils, cheeses, pastas (whole grain type), whole grain breads and whole grains should be eaten often. Also some good advice I haven't seen before is to eat big within two hours of bedtime and the body will retain these calories due to the inactivity during sleep. If indigestion is a problem, there are several good digestive aids on the market.

Nutritional companies market weight gain powders and chewable tablets that are sold in health food stores, as well as muscle builder powders and products for athletes. Weight gainers help the athlete to gain two or three pounds a week which is a safe weight gain. When gaining weight, exercise is important so that muscle and not fat is being formed. Since an unbalanced body chemistry usually accompanies weight loss, it is important to take a high quality natural vitamin, mineral, electrolyte supplement several times a day to help the body to gain weight and balance body chemistry. Electrolyte replacement (water soluble minerals) before and after exercise competition by using trace mineral drops or natural electrolyte drinks or tablets will help to avoid weight loss. Herbs to help weight gain, if needed, are Ginseng, Saw Palmetto and Sarsaparilla. These herbs have been properly combined in weight gain products that are sold in health food stores."

"While we're on the subject of food, Don, could we discuss carbohydrates? I know that many athletes today are eating them prior to competition or drinking carbo drinks. How effective is this?"

"Well, A.O., there are two types of carbohydrates; simple and complex. The sweet tasting ones are simple; such as syrups, white sugar, honey and there are some in milk products and beers. Some of the Carbo-fuel type drinks (not all) I've seen for athletes are made from fructose (fruit sugar) or sucrose (corn sugar). These are basically sugar water drinks that, while they may supply instant energy by raising blood sugar immediately, it will fall again within ½ hour or an hour and then many experience hypoglycemic or diabetic symptoms such as fatigue, weakness, shakiness and lightheadedness.

The complex carbohydrates; brown rice, potatoes, whole grain breads and cereals, pasta, vegetables, etc., provide the best nutrition. The fresh fruits are also good and healthy and they contain both simple

122

and complex carbohydrates.

Although simple carbohydrates stimulate insulin production by the pancreas which tells the body to make and store fat, they're not a good way to gain weight. This is because they increase blood fat (cholesterol and triglycerides) and uric acid which may cause gout and arthritis. Simple carbohydrates are poor nutrition providers. They actually reduce athletic endurance and may contribute to cardiovascular disease.

Small amounts of simple carbohydrates daily are OK, especially honey in place of white sugar. However, balance them out with larger amounts of the complex carbohydrates as mentioned earlier and protein (lean meats) and dairy products. Incidentally, a person requires approximately 60 grams of protein daily for each 120 pounds of body weight."

"Finally, Don, could we sum up the nutritional advice for the karate-ka?"

"Yes, thank you, A.O. The karate-ka should try to eat a balanced diet daily including raw fresh fruits, vegetables, complex carbohydrates, good quality protein lean meats and fish, poultry, milk, eggs, dairy products and high fiber foods. Always make sure meats are cooked well done to avoid parasite infection. Use a quality, natural vitamin, mineral, electrolyte supplement several times daily. Add additional supplements as required for individual needs, take power booster supplements two hours before competition and follow advice given earlier to build strong muscles, bones, blood, nerves and connective tissue. Drink plenty of pure water, get proper rest, avoid drugs, alcohol and tobacco, and exercise daily.

An herbal internal cleanse is important once or twice a year to keep the digestive system, small intestine and colon cleansed and functioning properly. Experts also now advise to use high fiber foods like unprocessed bran or psyllium very often to help prevent colon cancer (these fibers act like a broom on the colon wall).

Remember, since fluid replacement often means the difference between winning and losing to follow advice given earlier on how much to drink before and after competition. Electrolytes are water soluble minerals that the body loses when we perspire or urinate. It is important to replace these daily with trace mineral drops; sea salt and kelp are also mineral rich nutrients.

Every time we eat or drink we are contributing good or bad to our body chemistry. The food or drink we consume nourishes our blood, the river of life, that feeds all of our body's tissues and systems. If we do our best daily to consume only those things which are beneficial in proper amounts, we will prove that proper nutrition produces performance for the karate-ka and everyone else."

Note: This is nutritional, not medical advice. If you have a medical problem see your physician or health care professional, preferably one who knows nutrition; vitamins, minerals and herbs.

一、私達は、堅い精神を作るため心と体を訓練します。

一、武道の道を追求し常に正しい観念を持ちます。

一、気力を持ち、自分の弱さを捨てます。

一、礼儀を重んじ、目上の人を尊敬します。

一、神に従い、謙遜の徳を忘れません。

一、知恵と強さを求め、他の物は求めません。

一、空手の精神で、本当の道を追求します。

道 場 訓

Dojo Kun

Will train heart and body for a firm, unshaking spirit.

Will pursue the true meaning of the martial way so that, in time, our senses may be alert.

With true vigor, will seek to cultivate a spirit of self - denial.

Will observe the rules of courtesy, respect our superiors, and refrain from violence.

Will follow God and never forget the true virtue of humility.

Will look upward for wisdom and strength, not seeking other desires.

All lives, through the discipline of Karate, will seek to fulfill the true meaning of the way.

HANA-DAI ICHI KARATE ASSOCIATION
OF THE
UNITED STATES OF AMERICA

ソウチン型

Sochin kata

テクニック

techniques

空手に先手無し

Karate Ni Sente Nashi

"There is no first strike in karate."

Funakoshi

精神の抑制の無きものは、破
壊され壁の無い町のようだ

Author and Grandmaster Austin Box,
Karate-Do Seminar at Kansas City, 2001.

"He that hath no rule over his own spirit is like a city that is broken down, and without walls." Proverbs 25:28

武道では、
技を千日で学び、
それを万日磨く、
勝者と敗者は一瞬にして決まる。

"In Budo, it takes one thousand days to learn a technique, ten thousand days to polish it; the difference between victory and defeat is measured in a fraction of a second."

Samurai Maxim

Glossary

Applications	Bunkai
Attacker	Kataki
Attention stance	Heisoku dachi
Back fist strike	Uraken uchi
Back hand strike	Haishu uchi
Back kick	Ushiro geri
Back stance	Kokutsu dachi
Basic training	Kihon
Begin or start	Hajime
Board breaking	Shiwari
Body	Karada
Bottom fist strike	Tettsui uchi
Bow	Rei
Cat stance	Neko ashi dachi
Combinations	Renzuko
Crescent-kick block	Mikazuki-geri uke
Defender	Uke
Double forearm block	Morote uke
Downward block	Gedan barai
Drawback hand	Hikite
Elbow strike	Empi uchi
Exercises	Undo
Five step sparring	Gohon kumite
Flying front kick	Tobi geri
Forearm block	Ude uke
Fore fist straight punch	Seiken choku zuki
Forms	Kata
Forward stance	Zenkutsu dachi
Free sparring	Jiyu kumite
Front	Shomen
Front kick	Mae geri
Front snap kick	Mae geri keage
Front thrust kick	Mae geri kekomi
Half front position	Hamni
High level	Jodan
Hook punch	Kagi zuki

Hourglass stance	Sanchin dachi
Immovable stance	Fudou dachi
Inside block	Uchi uke
Junior	Kohai
Kiai	"feeling together"
Knee kick	Hittsui geri
Knife hand block	Shuto uke
Knife hand strike	Shuto uchi
Line up	Narande
Lower level	Gedan
Lunge punch	Oi zuki
Meditation	Mokusoh
Middle level	Chudan
One step realistic sparring	Jiyu ippon kumite
One step sparring	Ippon kumite
Open stance	Hachiji dachi
Outside block	Soto ude uke
Palm heel strike	Teisho uchi
Practice	Keiko
Punching	Tsuki
Ready posture	Yoi
Reverse punch	Gyaku zuki
Relax	Naotte or yasume
Riding horse stance	Kiba dachi
Roundhouse kick	Mawashi geri
Senior	Sempai
Side kick	Yoko geri
Side snap kick	Yoko geri keage
Side thrust kick	Yoko geri kekomi
Sit correctly	Seiza
Sparring	Kumite
Stamping kick	Fumi komi
Stomach	Hara
Stop	Yame
Straw-padded post	Makiwara
Traditional military greeting, "push"	Osu
Training	Renshu
Teacher	Sensei
Three step sparring	Sanbon kumite
Training hall	Dojo

Training uniform	Gi
U–punch	Yama zuki
Upper block	Jodan uke
Vital energy	Ki
Way	Do
X-block	Juji uke
Yes or ok	Hai

Counting in Japanese

One : Ichi (i-chi)
Two : Ni (ni)
Three : San (sa-n)
Four : Shi (shi)
Five : Go (go)
Six : Roku (ro-ku)
Seven : Shichi (shi-chi)
Eight : Hachi (ha-chi)
Nine : Ku (ku)
Ten : Ju (ju-u)
Twenty : Niju
Thirty : Sanju
Forty : Yonju
Fifty : Goju
Sixty : Rokuju
Seventy : Nanaju
Eighty : Hachiju
Ninety : Kuju
One Hundred : Kyaku

Black Belt Ranking

Shodan : 1st Dan
Nidan : 2nd Dan
Sandan : 3rd Dan
Yondan : 4th Dan
Godan : 5th Dan
Rokudan : 6th Dan
Shichidan : 7th Dan
Hachidan : 8th Dan
Kudan : 9th Dan
Judan : 10th Dan

Bibliography

1. Box, Austin. <u>Foot Fighting Empty Hand Way</u>. Colorado Springs, Colorado: Master Austin Box, 1980.

2. Burns, Donald J. <u>An Introduction to Karate for Student and Teacher</u>. Dubuque, Iowa: Kendall/Hunt, 1977.

3. Funakoshi, Gichin. <u>Karate-Do Kyohan: The Master Text</u>. Tokyo: Kodansha International Ltd., 1973.

4. Jennings, Joseph. <u>Personal Profile: Hidehiko (Hidy) Ochiai Spiritual Warrior</u>. Derby, Connecticut: Charlton Publications, Inc., 1974.

5. Motobu, Choki. <u>Okinawa Kempo: Karate-Jutsu on Kumite</u>. Olathe, Kansas: Ryukyu Imports Inc.,1977.

6. Nakayama, Masatoshi. <u>Best Karate Fundamentals</u>. Vol. 2. New York, New York: Kodansha International Ltd., 1978.

7. Plee, H.D. <u>Karate by Pictures</u>. London: W. Foulsham & Co. Ltd., 1962.

8. Taffel. <u>Graphic of Survey</u>. New York, New York: Oxford Book Company, 1960.

Index